AF265914
Where pizza dreams
met dusty trails,
Could teamwork win
when courage fails?

Rebel woke to a bright autumn morning,the air rich with dough and melting cheese.

Rooster puffed his feathers, eyes shining, watching the festival come alive.

Paw and feather, side by side, they raced toward a Grand Prix adventure.

1

This adventure belongs to:

Name: _______________________________________

Date: __________

Age: __________

If I could create my own amazing dish, I would invent:

____

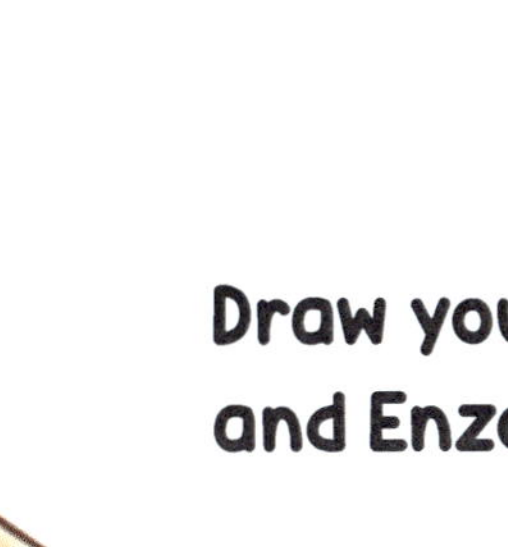

Draw yourself joining Rebel, Rooster,
and Enzo at the Pizza Grand Prix!

Rebel & The Rooster™
Pizza Grand Prix

Featuring Enzo

A tale of teamwork, dusty trails, and pizza dreams!

Written by Lou Basenese, Jr.
Illustrated by CIStudio
Published by Lou Basenese, Jr.

3

Dedication

Dedicated to my granddaughter, Eva Grace

Your bright, beautiful spirit reminds
me that the most precious
moments in life are the ones we share
together that are filled with laughter,
imagination, and love.

This story was written for you, and it will always be yours.

Author's Note

Rebel wasn't just a dog, he was Ed and Carole Nunnally's gentle giant, their furry alarm clock, and the keeper of every secret ever whispered into his floppy ears.

The rooster? Well, he thought he owned the place. And honestly, he kind of did.

Watching Rebel's kindness, his loyalty, and that tail that never stopped wagging inspired these stories. The adventures he shares with Rooster celebrate all the joy, courage, and laughter that animals bring into our lives.

These tales are a love letter to the pets who brighten our days and teach us, in their own wonderful ways, how to be better humans.

— Lou Basenese

PIZZA GRAND PR

The first rays of morning slipped over the hill,
With warm cheesy smells that made noses thrill.

Rebel jumped up, tail thumping the hay,
Rooster crowed loud, "It's Pizza Grand Prix Day!"

Each fall, this legendary race begins,
With racing karts and hopeful grins!

A scooter buzzed in, shiny and bright,
Kicking up dust in the golden light.

Enzo jumped off with a scarf in the breeze,
"Buongiorno, amici!" he called with ease.

Rebel barked loud, Rooster crowed with delight,
"Let's build a kart that will win tonight!"

PIZZA GRAND PRIX

Enzo spun circles, pretending to steer,
"The Pizza Grand Prix, the greatest race here!"

He waved his paws and zoomed all about,
His grin the biggest without a doubt.

Rebel barked, "Racing with pizza? Yes!"
Rooster squawked, "We must pass this test!"

PIZZA GRAND PRIX
GATTO
G

Soon children gathered near the pen,
From farms and homes, again and again.

"Teach us more!" they begged with glee,
Enzo held up a card to see.

"GAH-TOH!" he crowed, "That means cat!"
Kids meowed and giggled, crawling just like that.

PIZZA GRAND PRIX

Rebel drew a circle on the ground,
"Pizza!" he barked with a joyful sound.

Rooster scratched wheels and a crusty base,
"A pizza-kart racer to win the race!"

Enzo clapped loud, "Bellissima.....hooray!"
Their hearts revved up, let's build it today!

They searched the shed for parts to spare,
Old wheels, ropes, and wood to share.

They fixed Paolo Pig's ramp before it broke,
And gave Dottie Duck a crate, what helpful folk!

"Grazie mille!" called friends far and wide,
Helping felt warm with pals by their side.

The moon rose high as hammers kept their beat,
Three friends determined to complete their feat.

Rebel held boards steady, Enzo screwed them tight,
Rooster checked each bolt by lantern light.

Sparks danced upward through the starry air,
"Stupendo!" Enzo cheered with flair!

Dawn broke again, the kart ready to race,
Enzo jumped in with a grin on his face!

They pushed it down the gentle hill's grade,
A wobbly start, but not afraid.

It zipped, then CRASH!...a tumble and spin,
Laughing, they fixed it to race and win.

The track was dusted with flour so fine,
Lanterns hung high in a glowing line.

Karts lined up in a rumbling sound,
Engines revving, shaking the ground.

Mayor Goat bleated, "On your marks, start!"
"Andiamo!" they roared with racing hearts!

PIZZA GRAND PRIX

HONK! went the horn, they started like a shot,
Flour puffed up in a cloudy spot.

Then POP! went a wheel at the bumpy bend,
"Mamma mia!" yelped their racing friend.

"Pit stop now!" called Rooster with no delay,
Rebel barked, "Fix it fast, and we will win today!"

Paolo pig rolled up on his rattling cart,
"Take my tools, I'll help you restart!"

Dottie swooped down with a hook and twine,
"I'll grab that crate, you'll be just fine!"

Friends they'd helped came rushing near,
"We've got your back, we're all right here!"

"Avanti!" Enzo cried, they shot like a dart,
The pizza-kart thundered straight from the start!

Rooster shouted orders, his voice rang clear,
"Left at the hay bales! Sharp right...we're in gear!"

They blazed past fences, logs, and trees,
Racing ahead on the dusty breeze.

A flour sack swayed on a rickety beam,
About to burst, or so it would seem!

A gust blew hard with a sudden blast,
POOF! A white cloud exploded fast!

"Stay calm!" crowed Rooster. "Trust what we say,
Hold steady, Enzo, we'll find the way!"

"Turn left!" barked Rebel. "Hay bales ahead!"
"Straight on!" crowed Rooster through the powdery spread.

Kids waved bright flags as the path sharply curved,
"GATTO! GATTO!" they cheered and swerved!

The karts they'd helped slowed down, made way,
"Go, Enzo, go!" boomed loud through the fray.

35

Out of the flour, they blazed into sight,
The finish line close, one last burst of might!

WHOOSH! Past the hay bales, the final curve bent,
Every heart pounding, every ounce of strength spent.

They crossed the line as the crowd went wild,
"Campioni! We did it!" every voice smiled!

AMICI

As confetti drifted like cheese from the sky,
The farm lit up as the moon climbed high.

They shared their pizza, slice by slice,
While Enzo taught words warm and nice,

"Ah-MEE-chee means the friends so true,
Who stand beside you in all you do."

Fun Facts about
The Pizza Grand Prix

🌟 DID YOU KNOW? 🌟

🍕 Pizza Wasn't Always Round! Early pizzas came in all shapes; oval, square, even rectangle!

🔥 Blazing Hot Ovens! Traditional pizza ovens reach 800°F and cook a pizza in under 90 seconds. Talk about fast!

🌿 Pizza Colors = Flag Colors! Italian pizza uses basil (green), mozzarella (white), and tomato (red)—Italy's flag colors!

👩‍🍳 Pizza Pros Train Like Athletes! Master pizzaiolos spend years perfecting dough tossing, oven timing, and flavor balance.

🏁 Pizza Competitions Are Real! There are pizza-tossing contests, speed-making races, and creative topping championships!

🐾 Some Dogs Steal Toppings..... But Rebel would never admit it!

The Pizza Grand Prix Treasure Hunt!

Hidden throughout this story are secret clues from the race!
Can you spot them all?

Find These:

🍅 Tomato — Flavor power..........page 1

🌿 Basil leaf — Italian spirit..........page 8

🔥 Oven flame — Baking magic..........page 11

🍕 Pizza slice — Competition symbol..........page 37

🔧 Rolling pin — Dough prep tool..........page 40

🧀 Cheese curl — Mozzarella stretch..........page 31

🐾 Pawprint — Uh-oh! Rebel's been snacking! ....page 24

Your Results:

Total found: __________

Hardest to spot: ______________________________

My dream pizza toppings: ______________________________

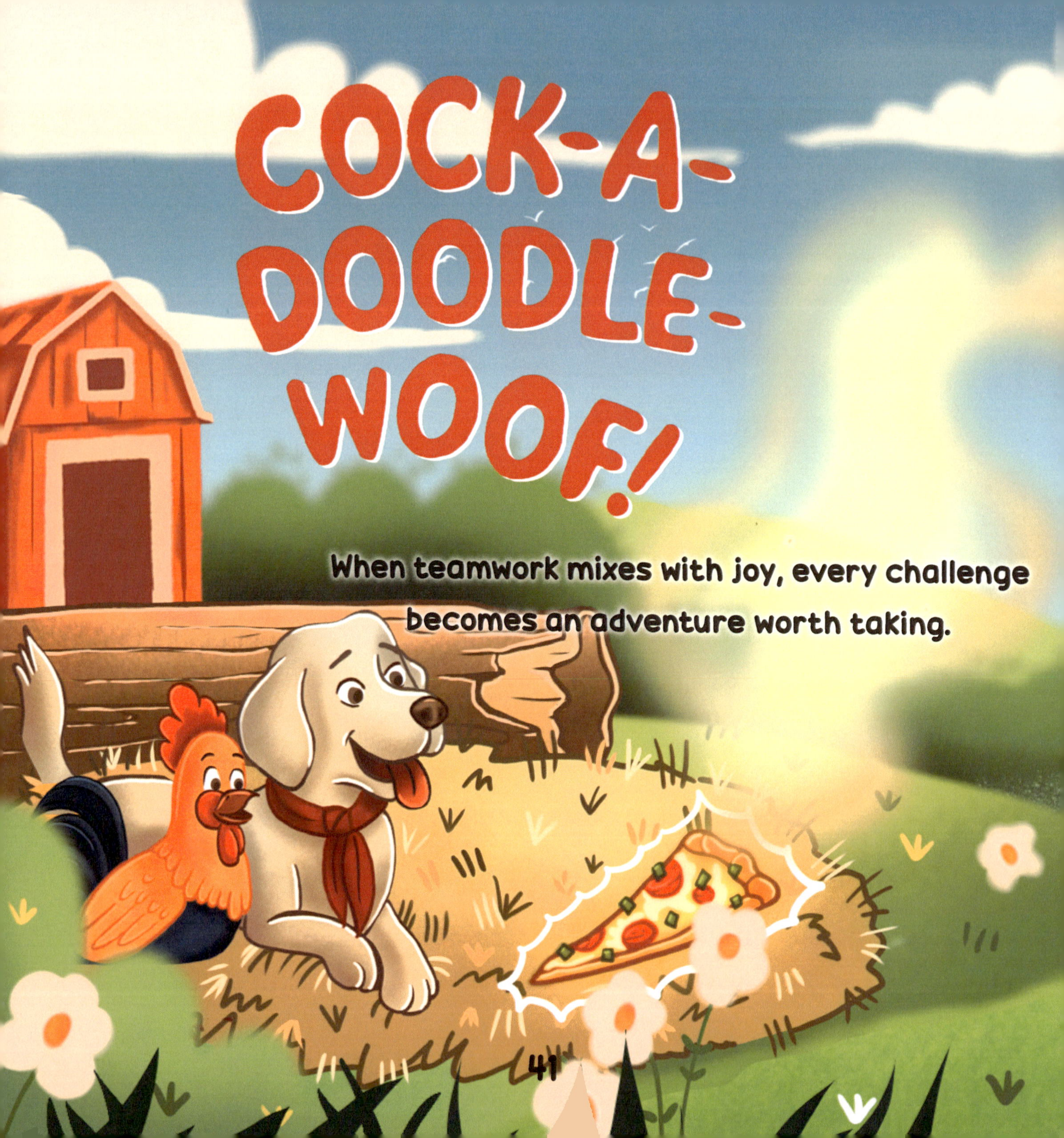

COCK-A-DOODLE-WOOF!
When teamwork mixes with joy, every challenge becomes an adventure worth taking.
41

Every great creation begins with imagination.

In the Pizza Grand Prix, victory was built
with courage, teamwork,
and the joy of trying something new.

Like rising dough,
bravery grows
one try at a time.

Until the next adventure,
— Rebel, Rooster & Enzo